COPYRIGHT NOTICE

For more information about *33 Things That Can Go Wrong (AND DO!) In Real Estate Transactions*; individual orders; bundled orders, discounts for bulk-quantity purchases; audio products; interviews; information on seminars; JV opportunities; mentoring/consulting; booking the author to speak at your next seminar, workshop or event; please contact the author at any one of her websites below.

www.SilvanaSarkis.com

www.SilvanaSellsHomes.com

DISCLAIMER: The information in this book is true and complete to the best of my knowledge. All recommendations are made without guarantee on the part of the author or publishing company. The author and publisher disclaim any liability in connection with the use of this information that applies to all states with some specific reference to California law.

ACKNOWLEDGEMENTS

I would like to thank my family, friends, mentors, clients, colleagues, real estate vendors and my strategic partners. Where would I be without you? Your help, support and guidance along my real estate journey wouldn't be what it is today and I thank you. I also would like to thank Bart Smith for inspiring me to write this book. Lastly, to my dad, I'm thinking about you up there.

DEDICATIONS

I would like to dedicate this book to all those looking to improve their real estate gains and performances by following what I mention anywhere in this book that might apply to their situations; to my past, current and future clients; my strategic power partners or any person who decides to pick up this book and read it so it can help them with their purchase or sale of their biggest asset ... their home!

This is also great for anyone, as well as my strategic power partners, to give to your mutual clients so the book can educate or prepare them for what's to come. To all of you, I dedicate this book, too! Now, let's get started!

MEET THE AUTHOR

SILVANA SARKIS

In 2005, Silvana started American Classic Realty & Mortgage as a real estate broker and she developed a team of 25 employees to generate up to half a million in revenues her 2nd year in business. In 2007, she shifted her company to what the market dictated and has helped over 100 distressed homeowners in closing their short sales on their homes. She continues to help distressed sellers in crucial situations in probate, divorce, foreclosure, and other distressed real estate sales. Besides her law degree, she is a #realtorwithaJD, a Certified Probate Real Estate Specialist (C.P.R.E.S.) and loves to work with elders. Silvana, has coached and mentored over 250 agents, loan officers, and sales teams in her broker firm. She has a fiduciary duty in serving her clients needs and over exceeds her client's expectations.

On a personal level, Silvana has a burning desire to travel. She has 3 nephews and one niece that she absolutely adores. One thing that nobody knows about Silvana, she competed at Arthur Murray dance school for salsa, cha-cha, rumba and swing and won for 2nd place. Silvana has the knowledge and experience but most of all she has the heart to help her clients with their real estate needs. She loves referrals and takes every client need and customizes a solution. She would love to help you, your family and friends.

TABLE OF CONTENTS

MESSAGE FROM THE AUTHOR

MISTAKE #5
NON-COORDINATED

MISTAKE #6
DETAIL ORIENTED

WRAP-UP & WORDS OF ENCOURAGEMENT

MESSAGE FROM THE AUTHOR

I'm super excited that you picked up my book. In this book, you will learn what to do when buying or selling a house.

I decided to write the book because I have seen so many people, family, friends, and clients make mistakes hiring unprofessionals that do not properly and thoroughly advise the consumer when buying a home.

I've chosen the word "perspective" as a title for each main topic I'll be sharing with you, because it is the "perspective" from different people and players in the real estate business that I wish to share with you such as real estate agents, buyers, lenders, title/escrow companies, inspectors, or anyone involved in the transaction of the buying and selling of a home.

Since it is an overwhelming process, I hope you will find value in reading my book and you will be ready to BUY or SELL your American dream home with confidence. I wish you all the best. You're always welcome to contact me or my team with any questions at:

www.SilvanaSellsHomes.com

C'mon, let's jump right into this book and learn 33 + things that can go wrong with real estate transactions!

PERSPECTIVE #1
BUYER MISTAKES

MISTAKE #1
HIRING THE REALTOR

Hiring the right realtor when you are the Buyer is Essential. Many people fail to realize how important it is to hire the "RIGHT" realtor. The buyer's agent is called "THE SELLING AGENT" (CONFUSING? I KNOW.) Everyone and their mother have a family member or friend who is a realtor. That is ideal as long as your family or friend has experience, is a professional and is good at what they do. I know people who will hire a person whom they've only been dating for a month. Really????

Some things to consider when choosing the right buyer's agent:

1. Is he/she licensed? You can go to dre.ca.gov to look up any realtor.

2. Does he/she have access to a MLS and will he/she send you property that is on the market?

3. Does he/she have his/her own e-Key (an e-Key is a way to give a realtor access to homes on the market)

4. Is he/she going to just show you the property immediately? Is he/she flexible?

5. Will he/she make calls immediately? Will they be assertive to get you access to the home?

6. Will he/she follow up?

7. Will he/she ask the correct question?

8. Does he/she have a strong personality?

9. Is he/she a good consultant and present good options?

10. Does he/she know the area or is he/she open to learning to get your questions answered regarding the area?

11. Is he/she fun to work with?

12. Would you refer him/her to your family or friends?

13. The most important question is: Is the realtor a PROBLEM SOLVER?

It is important to go with somebody who will have your best interest. The buyer does not pay for the commissions, it is actually the seller, so pick the best realtor (a.k.a. consultant) who has your fiduciary interest. You can interview 2-3 realtors but pick one that has expertise in negotiating on your behalf. Do NOT go with the Open House Agent or Listing Agent just because they are nice. Make sure they are qualified to fight on your behalf.

A buyer's realtor gets paid from the sellers listing contract with the listing agent. I have seen a buyer fall in love with a house but the buyer's agent does not want to negotiate because the MLS states that the seller will only pay 2% instead of 2.5% or 3%. This is sad because the agent is looking only at what benefits him or her and not the client.

THREE (3) PRIMARY DUTIES of hiring a great realtor are: #1) He/she should be a good consultant #2) Is he/she good at negotiating for your best interest? #3) Is he/she great in overseeing details?

BOTTOM LINE - MAKE SURE YOU PICK A GREAT BUYERS AGENT WHEN BUYING A HOME. A REFERRAL IS BEST!

MISTAKE #2
"PRE-APPROVED"

Are you pre-approved or pre-qualified?

The first step is to find a good loan officer? The best way is by referral? A great loan officer, whom we will talk about later, will be able to go over how much you are "Approved" for and submit the letter to your realtor. The pre-approval dictates your purchasing power. Pre-approval is a more detailed process than pre-qualified because it requires the clients to give the loan officer financial and personal information to obtain a credit score.

Some information that is required for a loan officer to get a borrower(s) pre approved is as follows:

1. Name, current address, phone number, email, social security number, work and other contact information

2. Credit report

3. 2-year tax returns

4. 30 days of previous pay stubs

5. Bank accounts with reserves

6. Any assets, home, pension or 401k

7. Down payment amount

The loan officer will then run a Desktop Underwriter (DU) or another automated program source to get a buyer qualified through Fannie Mae Guidelines. This can be used for conventional or FHA (Federal Housing Administration) loans.

I can't begin to tell you how many people I see who go to open houses without knowing what price they are pre- approved for. Please make sure you get pre-approved before you go house hunting.

GETTING PRE-APPROVED IS A MUST!

MISTAKE #3
LACK OF FUNDS TO CLOSE

How much money are you bringing to the closing table? Are you considering the down payment? Escrow fees? Title Fees? Other fees? Some people think all they have to do is bring the down payment. Wrong! The buyers are generally responsible for loan, escrow and title fees, which will also be discussed later in the book. The buyer does not pay for his realtor because that comes off the seller's gross profit. A buyer should ask the lender and escrow for a net sheet so they are not surprised and disappointed. It's good to ask for this upfront once you have a pre-approval letter. This will be an estimate and is subject to change based on the final purchase power and the vendor's fees that are chosen.

Funds to close can also be brought in through seller credits or a gift from a family member. Setting your expectations for what you need to buy the home is a necessity so there are no surprises. Also make sure that the closing money comes from the same account as the earnest money deposit. Asking the loan officer before depositing money to escrow is highly recommended. It will save you from another delay in escrow closing.

REMEMBER TO HAVE THE CORRECT AMOUNT OF MONEY TO CLOSE ON YOUR DREAM HOME!

MISTAKE #4
LIMITING THE SEARCH

What are you looking for? Who will be living with you? What city? What area? What square footage? How many bedrooms? How many bathrooms? Do you want a pool? Are you familiar with townhomes and condominiums and do you know that they have HOA (Homeowner Association) fees? It's also great to drive around during the day and night to check out the areas. Remember, this should be a fun process and a journey but it is truly your responsibility to do your own due diligence by asking questions and taking the time to get to know the different areas. BUYER BEWARE!

Sometimes the parties want different qualities in the home such as kitchen, bathrooms, closet space, great school districts, views, back yards, cul de sac, pool, etc.

You want to FALL IN LOVE! I have seen people start with 15 to 20 cities and then they'll go see homes and decide they don't like the area. It is a complete waste of everybody's time. Buyers should do their own research and limit the cities from 2 to 3 if possible. At the same time, do not be too analytical and indecisive so you can't make a decision. You do not want to create a paralysis of analysis. If you see more than 10 homes and they all start looking the same, it can get confusing. So, find something and if you fall in love with it -- GO FOR IT! I have seen many people enjoy the journey too much and then they realize they should have gone with the first home they saw. Remember limiting your search by doing due diligence but remaining flexible is the KEY TO YOUR HOME SEARCH!

Here is a Simple Checklist of what is important when you're searching:

1. City

2. Zip code

3. Specific Area

4. Bedrooms

5. Bathrooms

6. Living space in square feet

7. Lot Size

8. Pool

9. Any deal breakers

10. Do you need a View?

11. Garage?

DREAM BIG, BUT DON'T BE TOO METICULOUS WITH YOUR SEARCH!

MISTAKE #5
LACK OF COMMUNICATION

Have you ever lacked communication? When I first started doing real estate, I would always call or email my clients. Now with texting and social media, we have a different generation of buyers and sellers that want to do things differently. However, it's so easy to get misunderstood via text. I always try to call my clients for the big items or meet them in person to ensure there's no miscommunication between the clients and me. I always ask my clients how they prefer to stay in touch throughout the transaction process so we're always using their best channels of communication. When executing documents, we can review and sign digitally so we must be clear that all parties are comfortable with that way of signing.

Miscommunication arises also between the parties (e.g. husband and wife) and/or family members as well so I have to continue to create a great channel of communication with all pertinent parties. Sometimes, they want different qualities in a home so we have to make sure we are not only on the same page but working from the same book.

When clients are purchasing a home, they get excited and one of them or both may go shopping. I remind my buyers to not purchase any furniture, appliances or other big items before closing. This can affect your debt to income ratios for your loan (even though the lenders I work with also tell them that). I just like to remind them because it can be an overwhelming process and most clients are juggling work, kids, and their personal lives while they're also buying a home. It's great to have good communication with your clients even when they do not want to listen.

COMMUNICATION IS KEY!

MISTAKE #6
THE RIGHT HOME

Is this the right home? If so, why is it? Are you in love with the home? Does your partner like the home? What about the square footage? Is this the home that you are going to buy and sell? Is it for investment? What's your exit strategy? Will your kids be going to college and will you have to downsize? Sometimes, a buyer wants to buy a new development. If a buyer goes into a new development on their own, they are not going to be able to pick their own realtor and the builder and developer can require that they use the builder's lenders and other services. They also will want to sell you on upgrades and will say they are saving you money by giving credits but it's important that it is the home you want.

Asking them questions helps you understand what they like more. I always like to ask my clients when I'm showing them property, on a 1 to 10 scale (1 being the least and 10 being the best), how much do you like the property? Then I ask, why do you like it? What do you like best? What do you like the least? Are there any deal breakers with the home? Do you have any other questions? FInally are you ready to make an offer today? Asking these questions helps me understand more of what they are looking for and whether they are ready to commit to a home. As a buyer, you should have answers to these questions and have a game plan for the home you want to buy. BE CLEAR AND CONCISE ABOUT WHAT YOU WANT.

MISTAKE #7
THE RIGHT OFFER

What is the right offer? Sometimes we do not know until it gets accepted. Are you making the offer that is going to get accepted? I see so many people lose out on their dream home because of $10,000 or something as basic as a sink disposal or a toilet that doesn't work. Remember that you can gain equity when you buy at the right time. When you are buying a home for half of a million or three-quarters of a million -- GO ALL IN -- and make a fully-priced offer or accept the counter offer. I've seen many people lose out because they were stuck, mentally, on a price. Some people tend to think that they will get closing costs paid from the seller, although it's possible. When it's a competitive market, you have little or NO CHANCE. Your agent can write the offer for anything you request but really is that going to make or break you? Are you asking for too much? I write offers that my clients want me to write but I do my best to advise them of what I suggest they do when buying a house. I do it kindly and respectfully and then I'll negotiate the best offer for them.

The following terms are crucial but not the only terms when writing your offer:

1. Price

2. Close of escrow date

3. Financing; cash, conventional or FHA

4. Closing costs paid by seller

5. Any appliances included in purchase

Finally, as an agent, I seek to articulate to my client the best terms. The bottom line is this: WRITE YOUR HIGHEST AND BEST OFFER WHEN YOU LOVE THE HOME!

MISTAKE #8
TAKING THE CORRECT ADVICE

Who are you listening to? My mentor told me, "If you buy somebody's advice you have to buy their lifestyle." Think about this. If you are anticipating brain surgery, would you listen to your neighbor, plumber or even a family member who is not a brain surgeon? No! So why would you do that on the biggest transaction of your life? I know your family and friends love you, but you want to take advice from a professional who does this for a living and not one who has bought fewer homes or is not in the business.

If you have a qualified agent that is experienced, then have faith that they are going to give you their best advice. It's okay to ask questions but I always like to ask my clients to ask questions, and to be open for the answers. I make every effort to give them the best advice. Buyers should always proceed with caution and do their own due diligence especially when buying a home.

Sometimes, it's difficult to deliver the news and give advice but it is part of our fiduciary duty to be a consultant who includes communicating and educating on all options. I am the messenger and sometimes people get upset with the news I need to give them but, good or bad news, I will always offer options. A consultant will give great advice to you because that's why they are hired and paid.

REMEMBER THAT YOUR REALTOR SHOULD BE A PERSON YOU TRUST.

MISTAKE #9
PICKING YOUR BATTLES

What battles are you fighting? My mentor told me, "Do you want to be right or rich?" There are so many meticulous details when you are buying the biggest asset of your life - a home for you and your family. It's like a marriage. You must pick your battles.

Let me share a personal story. In 1987, my father's friend made an offer on a beautiful home for $110,000 in Anaheim, California. He did not purchase the home because of a roof that was falling apart, which would have cost approximately $10,000 to repair at that time. That was about 10% of the purchase price (a lot of money then). Well, that home is worth seven times that amount now. Although my father's friend thought he was making a great decision, was it?

Let me give you another example. I've had clients say, "I'm going to cancel if the seller does not fix this or pay for that." We are talking about a $500-$800 problem. Seriously, you're buying a home. What are you going to do when the AC stops working or the plumbing gets backed up? Home ownership is NO JOKE! Be ready and make sure you pick your battles wisely and take responsibility. I believe if you put your EGO aside, you can actually win in the long term.

MAKE SURE YOU'RE PICKING YOUR BATTLES FOR THE LONG TERM.

PERSPECTIVE #2
SELLER MISTAKES

MISTAKE #1
PICKING THE RIGHT REALTOR

When selling your home it's important to pick the "Right" realtor. There is a difference if it's a realtor who specializes in a specific home sale. For example, if you have a realtor who specializes in working with seniors, probate, foreclosure, short sale, REO (Real Estate Owned), divorce, downsizing, or upsizing. Some people hire their next door neighbor, a family member, or the realtor in the community. You have to hire somebody who specializes in the niche. For example, if someone is selling a home in probate-there are many things involved in a sale of a probate home depending on the estate. You want to make sure you hire a C.P.R.E.S. (Certified Probate Real Estate Specialist). I have this certification and a JD (Jurisprudence Doctorate) degree which helps BUT I ALSO have the experience of selling homes in probate. You want to hire a realtor that can overcome obstacles and is a problem solver.

Some Realtors have Senior Real Estate Specialist (SRES) designation, which means that they meet the special needs of senior Americans when selling, buying, relocating, or refinancing residential or investment. This is a realtor who wants to focus on helping seniors.

There are also agents who focus on divorce and have earned the title of Certified Divorce Real Estate Expert (CDRE) or Real Estate Collaboration Specialist-Divorce (RCS-D) or Certified Real Estate Divorce Specialist (CREDS).

Some agents, when foreclosures are very high, will earn their certification as a Short Sale Specialist and the designation for that is SFR (Short Sale and Foreclosure Resource Expert) or CDPE (Certified Distressed Property Expert).

Basically, you want to hire the specialist that's right for your situation. The bottom line is HIRE THE RIGHT REALTOR for your situation. It can make a big difference to ensure a smooth closing so use an agent that knows how to protect you when selling your home and getting you the highest price for your money.

MISTAKE #2
TAKING THE CORRECT ADVICE

Do you listen? Does your realtor listen? Is the home PRICED TO SELL! In my opinion, all homes will sell if you have the right price, marketing, and realtor.

Most homes DO NOT SELL for three primary reasons:

1) Price - The seller(s) believe that the home is worth a certain amount because of what their friends or family said or they compare it to a home that is not comparable because of size or proximity. Your realtor needs to pull comparables (sold properties within 90 days) for you in the area and help you determine a good price to sell the home. When my clients listen to me, my listings will be sold in less than two weeks.

2) Marketability - The home is not being marketed through different streams, including but not limited to, social media, open houses, flyers, Google Ads and many other marketing campaigns. Are you allowing the realtor to show the property and market the property on the Internet, a sign on the front yard, access to the home with a lockbox, social media, and other Internet advertising?

3) The realtor is not doing his/her job. Also, sometimes there are different philosophies between the parties and the listing agent. At the end of the day, a realtor needs to do his/her best

to articulate with skill, integrity the fiduciary duties and correct advice for their client(s).

Many times, I hear sellers comparing themselves to others who sold their houses and yet no situation or home is the same and of course TRANSACTIONS ARE NEVER THE SAME because people and homes are unique. Every transaction is handled differently depending on the situation.

Finally, TRUST THE PROCESS AND THE REALTOR.

MISTAKE #3
LACK OF COMMUNICATION

Communication as mentioned before in the buyer section is key! Whether it's you and the client or among the parties themselves, it's important to request how you want to communicate whether it's via text, email, phone, and social media. Sometimes the sellers are not speaking to each other and forget to address something with the realtor. In real estate, it's important to communicate and when there is miscommunication, things can get mixed up. It's important that everything gets addressed in the beginning so expectations are met.

COMMUNICATION IS KEY!

MISTAKE #4
LACK OF MOTIVATION

Why are they selling? Are they acting based on EMOTIONS OR LOGIC OR BOTH? Sometimes people lack the ability to continue fulfilling the purpose of listing their home. This has a lot to do with communication. Sometimes people get drained and they lose motivation. Sometimes when things get serious, they have a change of heart. Some sellers get stubborn because they did not get their way. Some sellers cannot find a suitable replacement property. Sometimes, one of the sellers will not allow the appraiser or other inspectors in the home and they are resistant, making excuses about allowing an inspector or appraiser into the home. At times, a seller loses motivation to sell because the job transfer does not go through or the marriage gets reconciled and the parties remain in the home. I always like to remind my clients why we started the process in the first place. Reminding them of their WHY will realign their focus and help get back on track.

I always like to ask my sellers, WHY ARE YOU SELLING?

MISTAKE #5
MISREPRESENTING

Sellers need to focus on representing the home and neighborhood. Sometimes they will misrepresent certain things about the home or neighborhood based on their own opinions. Sellers should represent facts only and not gossip or express opinions about the home.

Also, a listing agent should ask if the seller is up to date making payments on a mortgage, taxes, insurance, and Homeowner Association dues (HOA). At times, I have seen where the person is not on the deed but is acting as the seller without a power of attorney. If the person on the deed is no longer alive, then the listing must be made in the name of the estate and personal representative (PR) of the estate. We have to confirm that the person who actually signs the listing and all the documents is actually 100% authorized to sell the home.

ACT IN THE CAPACITY AS A LEGAL OWNER(S) OF THE HOME.

MISTAKE #6
NON DISCLOSURE

Sellers must disclose all hidden or unknown defects that materially affect the sale of the home, such as deaths within three years, any drugs, encumbrances, liens, permits and construction about the home. As an agent, I ask a lot of questions when I walk through the home with the seller. As I walk through every part of the home or rooms, I ask them if they have any information regarding each room in the house, the kitchen, the living room, and the bathrooms. I ask for any information regarding the plumbing, electricity, the air conditioner, the heater, the neighbors, the neighborhood, the Homeowners Association (HOA), the property taxes, any foundational problems or any other items that I need to know about the house. The more honest the sellers are with me, the better I can help them. I also will prepare my own visual inspection disclosure. I confirm that they have detectors for smoke and carbon monoxide and make sure the water heater is strapped. A good listing agent knows a lot about the home because they have asked the sellers all the questions about the home.

FULL DISCLOSURE IS A MUST WHEN IT COMES TO SELLING A HOME.

MISTAKE #7
PICKING YOUR BATTLES

You must pick your battles! Many times, I've seen sellers choose to be right vs. conquering the sale over meticulous issues. Both parties need to come in with a clean heart and a perspective that they want this house and they are going to do their part. Seller wants to sell the home and fix what needs to be fixed to get the home sold and buyers need to understand the year of the home and whether they really are buying only the dream of home ownership. It's sad to see people cancel escrow due to the fact that they insist on battling everything that comes up. I always look at obstacles as a way to grow a greater relationship with the client and together, as a team, we will overcome the obstacles we come across.

THE GOAL IS TO SELL THE HOME FOR THE HIGHEST PRICE, AS FAST AS POSSIBLE. AND HAVE A SMOOTH, BATTLE-FREE TRANSACTION.

MISTAKE #8
BEING CHEAP

Being Cheap is not a Great Attribute to have as a seller. Sellers want to know one thing, how much is this going to cost me? The biggest cost is commission. The seller is responsible for paying both an agent's and broker's commissions. Most listings are 5 to 6%. I have seen realtors come in and take a flat fee to sell a home or advertise as 1% or 1.5% listing and the seller doesn't realize that they still have to pay the buyer's agent. Also, what is that realtor doing for marketing? What corners are they cutting? Are they paying for ads? Are they paying for marketing the property? Are they experienced? YOU PAY FOR WHAT YOU GET!

Sometimes, a buyer wants a credit instead of making repairs. Sometimes, they are set on a certain price and they want an AS IS SALE and they don't want to renegotiate. I like to find out from my sellers what they are willing to negotiate and repair. A Good Story: I had a buyer who bought a home and there was a common wall that was falling apart. The buyer wanted $800 or he was going to cancel. The seller (not my client) rejected the offer and so I ended up giving him the credit because when emotions are high, intelligence is low so I rather not lose the property for my buyer and I prefer to give in and make it happen. My client's property five years later appreciated over $200,000. Imagine for $800, they would have lost the home they loved, which appreciated and would have continued to pay rent and not gain equity. I always consult and advise my clients saying let's pick our battles and not be cheap or meticulous about certain things. We have to focus on the big picture.

Sometimes, I see sellers who do not want to fix anything on the request for repairs, but I help them understand that they have been living there and they need to deliver a property to the buyer that is not broken. That's just the right thing to do! I always advise sellers that the termite report and clearance is the seller's responsibility. That is of course if the buyer is not a cash buyer and getting a discount on the price.

THE MORAL OF THE STORY IS - DON'T BE CHEAP!

MISTAKE #9
REPAIRS

Buyers will usually order a physical inspection and the buyer's realtor may request the seller to make repairs to the home before the close of escrow. The seller will choose to make the repairs. I have also seen where the buyer may request a certain amount of credits instead of making the repairs. The Request for Repairs form must be written by the buyer's agent and sent to the sellers (and their agent) within the general 17 day physical contingency period (in California). I always tell my buyers to make sure we do not make the list too long because small things are easy to fix by a handyman. If I am representing the seller, and depending on the seller, they may want to fix all the items because it's about taking pride in delivering a home in the best possible condition to the buyer. If they are elderly sellers, I will always find a handyman to fix things or we can do a credit back to clients towards closing costs.

MAKING REPAIRS IS NEGOTIABLE AND UNIQUE TO EACH HOME.

PERSPECTIVE #3
REALTORS

MISTAKE #1
INEXPERIENCED

Are you hiring the right realtor for you? A listing agent is the seller's agent and the selling agent is the buyer's agent. A realtor is a licensed salesperson by the Department of Real Estate (DRE). They also hold their title as "Realtor" because they are part of the Board of Realtors, California Association of Realtors (CAR if you are in California), and National Association of Realtors (NAR). I suggest you look up the person you hire on DRE and ask the person if he/she is part of the board. You can get your license and sell real estate but did you hang your license with a broker? Are you selling or buying? Are you in foreclosure? Are you in probate? Are you getting a divorce? Is your realtor a Certified Probate Real Estate Specialist (CPRES)? Does he/she have a Law Degree (Jurisprudence Degree)? Personally, I like to consider myself more of a consultant/adviser.

I am a Master Negotiator which means I negotiate all terms and conditions of the contract. Are you hiring somebody because they are your friend? I have seen realtors treat their friend like a friend and not a client. For example, if they are late or procrastinate in their personal life, no doubt they will do the same thing when they sell their home.

However, if you hire a friend and they are a professional, too, it can be a great experience. I have represented many friends and they are my clients but when it comes to representing them, I put my law school hat on and every vessel in my body wants to protect my clients. I consider myself a consultant or a Real Estate Specialist and I like to negotiate the best terms for my client with all of my capabilities as much as possible: #realtorwithaJD and #realtorwithaJDinCA

Another thing to consider is that you can look up anybody with the Internet and social media platforms. I always do my best to get testimonials from my clients, too, so I can share them with future clients.

So here are simple steps to take when hiring the right realtor:

1) Go to dre.ca.gov and look the person up. You can see how long he/she has been licensed. Make sure there are no disciplinary violations.

2) How many transactions has he/she closed in your general or specific situation?

3) Ask him/her for testimonials from other clients or look the person up online. Does he/she have an online presence, social media page, website, linked in, etc.? This will help you get to know your realtor before the interview. This is more of a gut decision and gives you confidence that you picked the best realtor for you and your family.

4) Does the realtor belong to a big brokerage or small boutique brokerage? Although I have a small brokerage, my education background and experience gives me credibility. Therefore, going with a name brand brokerage does not guarantee you will have a great realtor. Also, is the broker silent or in the office supervising agents?

5) One of the biggest problems I find with inexperienced realtors is they don't have the resources to deal with obstacles. For example, there may be a lien on a title, a problem with a loan, an extension of time or so many other reasons. What's more, they're not creative enough and rarely can they come up with a reasonable resolution.

If you did your research, got to review some testimonials and you asked those questions, you might feel in your gut that this is the right realtor for you.

IT CAN MAKE YOU FEEL MORE CONFIDENT THAT YOU MADE THE RIGHT DECISION WHEN PICKING THE EXPERIENCED REALTOR AND THE RIGHT ONE FOR YOU.

MISTAKE #2
LACK OF COMMUNICATION

Communication is the key! Is your realtor communicating? Is he/she listening? What form of communication is he/she using? Email text phone??? It's important that you instruct him/her to use the best form of communication including the relevant parties that make the decisions ...

Another thing I see is that people talk to the realtor and they verbally discuss the terms but don't read the contract or verify the information. Make sure what the realtor verbally discussed is the same as what the contract states.

Be assertive in what you need or ask the realtor. I have been told that the realtor was pushy or got upset or defensive. That always makes me wonder whose interests they are concerned about. Are they looking out for your best interest?

Lack of communication before you sign a contract to work with your realtor is a good sign to leave and find another realtor. If you have a binding contract to work with them then you have to cancel the contract. If you are a buyer, you were asked to sign a Buyer's Representation Agreement. A Buyer's Representation Agreement is a contract that states you will buy a home with that realtor.

AS A SELLER, IT'S CALLED A LISTING CONTRACT TO SELL YOUR HOME EXCLUSIVELY WITH THAT SELLER.

MISTAKE #3
CONFLICTING PERSONALITY

Can you get along? It's like being married when you're buying or selling a home. Make sure you actually like them. Will they make the experience fun yet professional? Do they have an awesome way of articulating the options available to you?

Will they be able to negotiate ethically and diligently with a smile? It's important that they have a smile on their faces and optimistic attitudes even when things aren't in the preferred direction. They must listen to what you need and want in the home or terms and negotiate on your behalf.

A great realtor is also a problem solver. I remember working with several clients when it was like a rollercoaster, in and out of escrow five times in one day. Patience is a virtue.

A great realtor also oversees the details in the transaction. This has a lot to do with their personality and if they are organized, prepared, and ready. I remember my mentor telling me that good is the enemy of great and I think a great realtor definitely needs to have a win-win attitude.

THE BOTTOM LINE IS TO HIRE A REALTOR THAT HAS A CONSULTANT MINDSET AND YET SOMEONE YOU WILL ENJOY WORKING WITH WHO GETS THE JOB DONE!!!

PERSPECTIVE #4
LENDERS

MISTAKE #1
NOT PROPERLY QUALIFIED

Most people have to obtain a loan from the bank. The loan officer works for the bank and represents the client to obtain financing for the home. This is as important as picking the realtor and sometimes it's a great idea to go with the realtor's power partner lender because they work together. It's important to pick a professional loan officer. I have worked with great loan officers who call me back immediately and consistently give me updates.

I always like to ask if they run the necessary Desktop Underwriting (DU) program. **DU** is an automated **approval** system that calculates whether a loan meets Fannie Mae or, in some cases, Federal Housing Authority (FHA) loan requirements. A **DU** evaluates a borrower's risk of delinquency by comprehensively evaluating several risk factors. Once the loan officer and processor package all your documents it goes to Underwriting. This has to be packaged very well since the underwriter is like the Judge for the lender.

The **underwriting** process leads to a decision as to whether a **loan** will be approved. The term "**underwriting**" refers to the process that leads to a final **loan** approval or denial, which is determined by a professional **underwriter**. Many factors are at play in a lender's final decision on a mortgage **loan**. The underwriter critiques the property, the buyer, debt to income and loan to value ratios, and the package and he/she gives it the final approval. The underwriter gives it to the funder which is required before the loan is funded. The funder also wires the loan amount to escrow and the file is prepared for closing. The buyer will also have to wire the down payment and closing costs to escrow before we close and record. EVERYBODY plays a big role and we must have a win-win attitude, remain flexible, and have consistent communication.

MISTAKE #2
NECESSARY DOCUMENTS

The loan officer will require the buyer to provide the following documents:

1. 2 years tax returns

2. W-2

3. 30-day pay stubs

4. 60-day bank statements,

5. Driver's license, ID

6. 401k or pension statements or other asset

The loan officer will also take a full loan application. The lender may also require additional documents but not limited to the 1) Verification of Employment (VOE), 2) Verification of Rent (VOR), 3) review of appraisal which is ordered by the bank, 4) preliminary report and any other reports or documents it deems necessary to finance the buyer's loan. It's good to get all these documents upfront and not wait until the last minute to avoid surprises.

A great loan officer will walk their client step-by-step through this process and it's important that the clients provide all the documentation required of the loan officer in a reasonable timeframe to avoid any delays. PROVIDING DOCUMENTS IN A TIMELY, SENSITIVE MANNER IS CRUCIAL.

MISTAKE #3
MARKET SHIFT

TIMING is everything when it comes to the market. There are many factors that affect the rates, which could cost the buyer to have to pay for the best rate. The economy and the stock market have a big impact on rates, credit points or costs. Once the customer finds a home and the loan process starts, that is when the loan officer can lock in the loan.

A lender can lock the rate usually for a 30 to 60 day period. I always recommend a minimum 45-day LOCK IN RATE just in case so the buyer does not have to pay for rate lock extensions. There are times when the loan officer locks the rate in and then the rates drop. That's a chance that you have to take.

If the rates drop, you lose the opportunity to relock but if it goes up you're locked at that low rate. It is definitely a risk when rate locking is involved but a great loan officer has to make the best decision for the client based on their experience, knowledge, and the market shift.

If the rate goes up and the loan officer has not locked the rate, this can mess up the debt-to-income ratios and it can possibly cause a person not to be pre-approved.

Disasters such as fires can also affect the market and homes from closing due to an insurance company unwillingness to insure the property because it's a risk.

THE MARKET CAN TAKE A SHIFT SO YOU NEED TO BE READY TO MAKE THOSE DECISIONS WHEN BUYING A HOME.

PERSPECTIVE #5
INSPECTIONS / PROPERTY

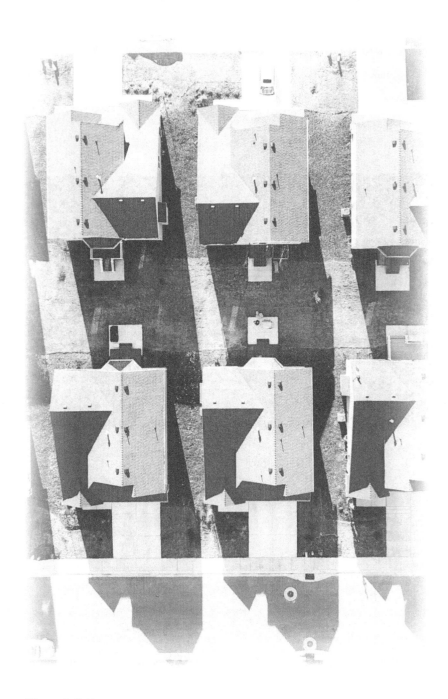

MISTAKE #1
PHYSICAL INSPECTION

Every buyer SHOULD have a physical INSPECTION of the property by a legitimate 3rd party company. When I am representing the buyer, I pick a professional company known by many in the industry. The buyer can also choose their own inspector. The inspection and report costs the buyer approximately $350 to $550.

The report is usually 50 to 60 pages and the inspectors will have a summary of the report on the first page, which includes the recommended repairs. The buyer will pay for the report out-of-pocket and will review the report with the inspector and buyers realtor. Sometimes, if a buyer is an investor or contractor, they will waive the inspection but I will have them sign a waiver of inspection. I always advise buyers to pay for an inspection and get a report for their own records. I like to order this the first week we open escrow because it tells us more about the home and we will make reasonable requests for repairs to the seller. I have seen times when an inspector can alarm the buyer and the sale is cancelled. Here is a story:

I once had a dual representation with one of my agents and a buyer. The buyer decided to pick his own inspector. Since they had the right to do so, the inspector went through the home and the seller came home early because he was an elder man and wanted to rest.

The inspector ridiculed the seller's home in front of him and I could not stop him because my buyers were there and they personally hired him. It made things very uncomfortable for all parties and he ended up telling them to check the foundation.

The buyer then spent another couple hundred of dollars on another inspector who checked the foundation and that specialist told the buyers that the inspector did not know what he was talking about. When the first inspector gave me his card, I looked him up and checked his license. He was no longer a contractor unlike his business card. It was an awkward situation so be very careful should you hire an inspector.

In this case, the buyers basically panicked, spent more money, and did not get a good inspector. We ended closing on the property but it was anxiety for the buyers and not a great experience.

ALTHOUGH A BUYER GETS TO CHOOSE AN INSPECTOR, IT'S BEST TO GO WITH A PROFESSIONAL AND A TRUSTED COMPANY FOR YOUR HOME INSPECTION.

MISTAKE #2
APPRAISAL VALUE

The appraisal is a person who tells the lender what the home is worth based on his findings. The buyer pays for the report. The lender orders it because they have an interest to ensure the home is valued at the purchase price.

Before the appraiser goes out to inspect the property, the seller is responsible to make sure that the home has the following:

1. smoke detectors

2. carbon monoxides detectors

3. Strapped water heater

If the value comes in lower than the purchase price, either the purchase price is renegotiated between the parties or the seller can provide comparables and contest the appraiser or the buyer to come in with more money to make up for the value.

STORY: I was representing the buyer when the appraisal came in lower. I went back and renegotiated and appealed the appraisal while my lender asked for comparables. We got them and the buyer received a $13,000 discount. YAY! Is it a unique home? Sometimes a home is so unique that it is hard to find a comparable so the appraiser has to do more research to analyze the value of the home.

The appraiser takes measurement and confirms the size with city permits if needed. If a home is misrepresented by size or condition, a second review may be requested. If the appraisal value comes in higher than the purchase price, the buyer and lender are content and it all moves along with escrow. The seller does not need to see the appraisal report unless it comes in lower and we are now renegotiating the price. If the appraisal comes in higher, you're buying an appreciated home and that is awesome. If the appraiser asks for repairs, the seller will then have to make them and the appraiser will have to come back and reinspect to make sure the repairs were made. Most of the time, the buyer has to pay for the reinspection, which is about $100 to $150.

The appraiser can request repairs on his report. Appraisers will usually call the seller's agent (listing agent) to make the appointment. IF THE BUYER IS PAYING FOR THE HOME - ALL IN CASH - NO APPRAISAL IS REQUIRED UNLESS THE BUYER WANTS ONE FOR HIS OWN RECORDS.

MISTAKE #3
TERMITE REPORT

What is a termite report? A termite report determines if there is any evidence of a wood-destroying insect. A seller will usually order a termite report for the buyer. The seller generally pays for it. Buyers can request fumigations and repairs and it is customary for sellers to make repairs but sellers are NOT required by law. This can be waived but when I am representing, especially a buyer, I request, on the purchase contract, an inspection, a copy of the report, and Section 1 clearance as well.

I usually order it when I get a listing too so we can prepare the seller with costs. The cost is always negotiable but sellers usually pay for Section 1. Section 1 items typically fall into the closing costs for the seller, meaning sellers pay for these treatments. This includes the cost of remediation, like tenting or spraying to eliminate an active termite infestation. It also means paying for things like repair of dry rot or wood that has been chewed by termites. Termite inspections and reports are an essential part of the real estate purchase.

HOMEOWNERS SHOULD MAINTAIN THEIR HOMES FREE OF TERMITES BY HAVING YEARLY OR 2-YEAR INSPECTIONS.

PERSPECTIVE #6
ESCROW / TITLE

MISTAKE #1
TITLE REPORT

Did you review the title report? The title report is ordered from a professional Title Company that ensures and protects the clients. The seller's agent is the person who generally orders the title report (aka preliminary report). The title report is reviewed by all parties and we cannot close until we have a title clearance. Many people such as both listing and buyers agents, along with the title representative, title officer, and escrow officer will review the document.

Here are a few things that show up on a title report against the seller or the property:

Loans – The majority of the time, sellers have a loan(s) and this will be paid off when the home is sold and escrow closes. Sellers will need to provide the mortgage statements. If a mortgage payment is not made in four months, the lender will file a NOD (NOTICE OF DEFAULT) and start foreclosure proceedings.

Tax Liens – The seller or anybody on the deed that has a lien with IRS, FTB, or county taxes will have to pay for these. Sometimes, this process can take up to 45 to 60 days to get payoff and it can delay escrow.

Child Support or Alimony Liens – If a seller has back payments on any child support or alimony liens These are also required to be paid off through the closing of escrow.

Vesting – How did the seller hold the title? Was he/she married or single because how title is held is important especially when somebody dies or gets a divorce. It can turn into a complicated situation in which the title officer will assist. Death certificates and divorce decrees may also be required to remove a name from the title.

Other encumbrances – I have seen easements, Homeowners Association city liens, and other contractor liens on property and they must all be negotiated and paid off through escrow.

I had clients who were upfront and honest who had 3 to 4 liens on the property and they ended up providing documents and it was sufficient to remove the liens on title before we were in escrow. However, there are also times when the seller will not know that there is a lien on the property and then when we order the preliminary report, they deny the lien, and the title company runs a document called Statement of Fact. Now we spend more time to find out if there is a lien creating more delays. Sometimes, liens can take 30 to 45 days to take care of it. THE CLEANER THE TITLE - THE SMOOTHER THE TRANSACTION.

MISTAKE #2
ESCROW DOCUMENTS

Most, if not ALL, transactions go through escrow. Escrow is the 3rd party that stays NEUTRAL to all parties. If I am the seller's realtor, I always go with a reputable and trustworthy escrow company. Most escrow fees are standard. Be cautious of escrows that are charging a lower rate or not insured or do not have a physical building (virtual). I also know some brokers that have their own escrow companies but I feel they can't be neutral when they incentivize their agents to use their escrows.

As a client, you have a right to ask questions and inquire. Escrow prepares the escrow instructions, grant deed, affidavit, other deeds, amendments, loan documents and any other documents required by the lenders title and the clients. One of the most important documents that I request from escrow to go over with my clients is the Estimated Fee Sheet (aka HUD Statement) because when it comes to fees, I would like to make sure my clients have no surprises at the end of the day.

Also, most clients like to walk into the escrow office to review, sign, and notarize the required documents. I like to pick an escrow company that I can trust but is close in proximity to me so I can always pick up documents and take it to my clients if needed. If I am representing the sellers, I always pick the escrow company.

My #1 goal is to make sure we have the right documents prepared, ordered or signed in a reasonable time.

TIMING IS CRUCIAL AND SO IS PICKING YOUR ESCROW OFFICER AND ESCROW COMPANY.

MISTAKE #3
FEES

If I had a penny for every time this question comes up - Who pays for what? - I would be rich. Fees can be complicated depending on who I am representing.

The seller usually pays for the following:

1. Both realtor commissions

2. Escrow fees

3. Title insurance and title fees

4. Termite report (and sometimes clearance)

5. Payoff demands

6. Buyers home warranty policy

7. All prorated taxes and insurance

8. Natural Hazard Disclosure Report

9. Homeowners Association fees

10. County or city fees

11. Recording fees and other miscellaneous items

These fees usually total the commission (approximately 5 to 6%) plus approximately 1% of the purchase price. I always like to overestimate and sometimes it's less and my clients are happy. Buyers usually pay for the following:

1. Any lender fees to obtain financing

2. Title fees

3. Escrow fees

4. Notary fees

5. Other miscellaneous fees where each fee comes from a different source. Your lenders fees need to be negotiated with the loan officer. Once again, it's usually lender fees plus approximately 1% of the purchase price for escrow title and other fees. Buyers usually pay for an appraisal fee and home inspection fees out-of-pocket at the time inspections are done.

MISTAKE #4
LACK OF COMMUNICATION

Picking the right title and escrow company is essential. A title gives you a report, and usually if everything is clean, you're good to go. If we have lines or other problems to remove from the title, a title officer, a title representative, and their team are essential to resolve the problem. Title requires certain documents to remove liens so you can move toward closing. Also, I've had times where my title representative will go with the client to record the deed or deliver a required document to assist with the closing.

Escrow is a NEUTRAL party but it is very important since they are the party that needs to communicate with all parties to get the transaction moved to the next phase.

Escrow has to communicate with the following:

1. Both realtors and their assistants or transaction coordinators.

2. Both buyers and sellers

3. Communicate with lenders, and their team, including but not limited to, loan officer, processor, underwriter, and funder

4. Communicate with the title representative, title officer and their team

Escrow officers have their own team to communicate with as well.

COMMUNICATION IS CRUCIAL FOR ALL PARTIES.

MISTAKE #5
NON -COORDINATED

Coordinating the documents is so important especially because time is of the essence. Escrow needs to coordinate:

1. Sending out escrow instructions to both buyers and sellers

2. Coordinate sending out crucial transfer documents to sellers

3. Coordinate pay off documents from the current seller's lender

4. Coordinate loan document signing times for the buyers loan documents with the lender and buyer(s)

5. Coordinate funding with buyers' lenders

6. Coordinate with title to confirm recording

7. Contact lien holders

8. Contact a homeowners association for documents and payoff demands

Coordination is required for a complete closure of a home sale. When all involved are communicating and they are doing their part, it's a win-win situation. Most clients do not see what goes on in the background but if someone slips, it really affects all the parties. Picking your power partners is essential to have a smooth transaction. Of course, there are always times when things get out of our control and we can't control them but it's great when all working for the same purpose to further and close the transaction for the Clients.

THAT IS THE WHOLE POINT AND HAVING A COORDINATED ESCROW OFFICER IS PREFERRED!

MISTAKE #6
DETAIL ORIENTED

Buying and selling houses requires overseeing details. As a broker and law school graduate, I look at every document, every report with laser eyes and I can quickly catch a problem and address it. I am a firm believer that if it's my clients, I am responsible for looking at all the documents. All the documents and reports are important to read and review but besides the buyers offer a Residential Purchase Agreement (RPA), the #1 important document. In my opinion it's the Preliminary Report for the seller. It can create so many delays that could prevent closing.

FOR THE BUYER, The #1 important document besides the accepted offer are the FINAL LOAN DOCUMENTS AND THE FINAL ESTIMATED STATEMENTS because they will address the buyers mortgage payment, what they need to bring as a down payment and closing fees. I address these documents with my clients before this stage to prevent last minute obstacles. If you have a great realtor, and they work with an amazing title and escrow team, then we will all work together to catch any missing piece of the puzzle and correct it provided we are overseeing the details.

WE MUST BE DETAILED-ORIENTED TO OVERSEE THE TRANSACTION DETAILS.

REAL ESTATE
MISTAKES WRAP-UP

SILVANA SARKIS

REAL ESTATE BROKER

REAL ESTATE MISTAKES WRAP-UP & WORDS OF ENCOURAGEMENT

Now that you have read through all of the mistakes and actions that real estate agents, buyers and sellers do and don't do, I hope you understand how hiring the best realtor who has a great team and personality is so crucial for your success when purchasing or selling a home.

Having the right team by your side that will solve problems and overcome obstacles will save you time and money but also make the journey a great experience.

I hope this book has given you confidence to understand the different perspectives you'll face and what to expect when buying or selling a home through every step.

Now, it's time to GO BUY YOUR AMERICAN DREAM HOME or sell the one you have. I wish to congratulate you in advance on purchasing your future home.

Genuinely,

Silvana Sarkis

Silvana Sarkis, JD
Real Estate Broker
SilvanaSellsHomes.com
#RealtorwithaJD